poems — *Jeff Rath* 5/09

# In the Shooting Gallery
## of
## the Heart

Jeff Rath

# In the Shooting Gallery
## of
## the Heart

Poems
by
Jeff Rath

Iris G. Press
Wrightsville, PA
www.irisgpress.org

## In The Shooting Gallery of the Heart

Copyright © 2009 by Jeff Rath

All rights reserved. No part of this book may be reproduced, in any form, without permission from the publisher, except by a reviewer who wishes to quote brief passages.

Cover Photograph by Adam Cowan

Cover Art Collage: *In the Shooting Gallery of the Heart,* by Adam Cowan and Jeff Rath

Published in the United States by

Iris G. Press
Wrightsville, PA

www.irisgpress.org

ISBN:0-9785858-4-4

for

Le Hinton – the brother I always wanted;

Rebecca Gonzalez – for her poetry, her heart,
her inspiration;

Richard Rath – my father

# Contents

### PART I: In the Shooting Gallery of the Heart

- 15 Something About the Moon
- 16 The Night Watchman
- 17 Steel
- 18 Dark Mullahs
- 19 A 12-Step Guide to Assimilation
- 22 The Legacy of Fire
- 23 Laundry as Life #1
- 24 black cadillacs
- 26 The Shooting Gallery of the Heart
- 28 Sixty Years of Mondays
- 30 Greenhouse Battleground
- 31 Laundry as Life #2
- 32 Sedna
- 33 Unfinished
- 35 Parent Trap
- 36 *Kristallnacht*
- 38 Love and Music 1: Blue Notes

### PART II: The Boilermaker's Daughter

- 43 The Boilermaker's Daughter
- 45 The Boilermaker's Daughter Speaks of Madness
- 46 Valediction of the Boilermaker's Daughter
- 47 The Boilermaker's Daughter Speaks to Her Son from the Other Side
- 49 The Boilermaker's Daughter Speaks to Her Daughter on the Other Side
- 51 Epilog: In the Wake

### PART III: Ghost in the Hallway

- 55 At 3 O'Clock in the Morning
- 56 Lorca's Daughter
- 57 Sleeping with the Muse
- 58 Duet for Cello and Piano
- 59 Land and Sea
- 60 Ghost in the Hallway
- 62 Love and Music 2: Duet

## PART IV: Dismantling a Life

- 65  Artist's Statement
- 67  Wedding Portrait—1971
- 69  Cat's Cradle
- 71  Title Search
- 73  In the Grotto of the Saint
- 74  The Dealer
- 75  No Such Place as Here
- 77  Expedition
- 79  Monument
- 80  Laundry Service
- 82  Reckoning
- 84  Blue Trucks
- 85  The Stone Witch
- 87  Prelude
- 88  The Star of Film Noir
- 90  Pirate
- 91  Pictures
- 93  Yeti
- 95  Weather Report
- 96  Stopped Clocks
- 98  Home
- 99  Inside the Mirror
- 100 Love and Music 3: Casualties
- 101 Risks
- 103 Son
- 105 Dismantling a Life

**In the Shooting Gallery
of the Heart**

**PART I:**

**In the Shooting Gallery
of the Heart**

"…nudging the small red ball of the soul
past the luminous clock dial of the night
toward some ill-defined vision of eternity."

## Something About the Moon

Despite all we have learned about the moon,
something in that cold ivory ball
still spins inexplicably
inside the heart's busy chambers.

Something in that lazy eye
rolling around in the black socket of the sky
conjures up smaller terrified eyes
seeking protection
against the random violence
of the predator's night.

Something of mystery
haunts the bold silver of its patient gaze—
it is a voyeur,
the silent witness.

Something causes dogs to bark
and pulls at all the dark tides
without and within.

Its music—
more felt than heard—
is still trying
to tell us something about ourselves we forgot.

What is it saying
that dogs still can hear
but we cannot?

## The Night Watchman

One night
the lights in the dream factory
will go out forever—
the solemn whistle bawling its news
across the village of your sleep.

At that moment
the timekeeper's clock will stop,
signaling the end of your shift.

Perhaps you will stir, lifting your head
to unconsciously mumble one final request
from beneath the comfortable sheets
of your bed.

In the instant all connections unravel,
you cease being the night watchman
and finally become the dream.

**Steel**

None of us believes
anything in life lasts as long as the steel
forged from these flaming metal rivers
barrel-assing out of the furnace mouth
and sluicing off to China or Japan
or wherever we're selling good ol' American technology
and sending jobs to these days.

We'd like to believe as our fathers did
that our jobs, like steel, will be here til we die,
but we aren't naive.
Maybe that's why we drink too much,
why our marriages stink—
because nothing in life ever lasts as long as steel.
Except disappointment.

If they could hawk disappointment on Wall Street
we'd all be millionaires,
and steel would mean nothing at all to us,
but in a different way.

## Dark Mullahs

Crows rock atop telephone poles
dark mullahs whose cawing
much like calls to prayer
echoes ancient cadences.

One drops through air
and gliding by
blinks
fixing me like a vision
in the eternity of its golden eye.

## A 12-Step Guide to Assimilation

1-
Pray your skin tone is close enough for you to pass.

2-
It is good if you already speak the language,
better still if you speak with no discernible foreign accent.

3-
As quickly as possible
buy into their mythology of success.

4-
In order to fit in,
you must sweep beneath the carpet of The Common Good
any facet of individuality.

5-
You must be willing to embrace
a collective ignorance,
and adopt an air of smugness
in order to disguise it.

6-
Accept the premise that there is only one god—
created in their image—
who loves only them,
who has blessed their leaders
with sacred vision,
and guides them on their holy mission
to destroy any and all
who threaten to weaken the covenant
they keep with their maker.

*7-*
You must continually forgive
those who lie, who cheat,
who persecute you—

after all, it is their country.

*8-*
You must be constantly grateful
they let you in,
and to show your gratitude,
you must be willing, at a moment's notice—
especially in times of strife—
to question the loyalty
of those like you,
to burn their churches,
to break their windows,
to harass their children
on their way to school.

*9-*
No matter how galling,
you must follow their rules,
and yet be prepared for the fact that
deep in their hearts
they will neither fully accept you
as one of them,
nor allow you to marry their daughter.

*10-*
Try to forget that you watched your father's face
as he was shot,
that you saw his bullet-vented body
dropped into the hole
the soldiers forced him to dig.

11-
Try not to dwell on the torture of your brother,
or on witnessing the rapes
of your mother and sisters
first by the rebels
then by the government troops.

12-
Finally, lock away deep in your heart
the truths of your history.
These people are not interested
in the messy details of your struggle—
unless, of course, you are a guest speaker
from a foreign country
visiting one of their churches.

## The Legacy of Fire

In fire's aftermath
we are obliged to learn
how everything precious to us
has the capacity to burn.
And even those objects
that remain intact
are transformed,
are denied the context
of their existence:
without the theater of a house,
the familiar setting of a room,
they become merely
another type of ash.

## Laundry as Life #1

The first mistake you made
was in thinking that life
was like a clothesline
with the shirts and towels and underwear
hanging in some logical order
beginning at the post
beside the porch
and stretching to that maple tree
rising majestically on the horizon
at the far edge of the yard.

### black cadillacs

black cadillac midnight
uptown five spot shoes

quarter til two
half past three allnight jamsession
bandstand royalty groove

so what
what's new
handy's troubled babies
all them dizzy bent axe tunes

uptempo altar
williamsburg bridge
saxophonequarternote moon

short change
no pay record label
strange fruit smokeyroom nights
jive-ass jukejoint roadhouse dues
trashcanalley fights

upright mingus
bird takes flight
lady sings mean to me
monk's moody fingers
gouge ebony notes from ivory keys

camelsandluckiesandcorktipkools
milesandcoltraneandcannonball
neoncolored counterpoint
solo trumpetblues

take five
stay alive
mainline spikes
expresslane dreams

eightballsandmaryjane
nowhere streetlight pain
shithouse shootinggallery nod

not even sleek black cadillacs
can take you all the way to god

## The Shooting Gallery of the Heart

In the shooting gallery of the heart
there are doors they warn you not to enter
before you check your soul in the alley way.
And there are windows
at street level
where you must jump up
to splatter your despair
for all to see
on the littered isthmus
of the sidewalk.

In the shooting gallery of the heart
women pretend to be asleep
when you roll against them in the night,
and your manhood shrivels each time
they touch your thigh and whisper "don't."
That pistol you keep beneath your pillow
goes soft, too, all its rage drains away
leaving a stain on the sheet
where only danger should have been.

The carnival has come to town,
all noise and lights and barkers bawling,
accusations flying,
illusions falling:
>"...*ring toss and chuck-a-luck,*
>*Hurry now...step right up...*
>*she walks, she talks, she fillets your heart*
>*and cooks it up before your eyes...*"

And you are happy to eat
that blackened meat,
its bitter tangled strands
trapped between your gnashing teeth.
As you spit out bits of buckshot
with every galling bite,

you learn to prize those tiny balls of bloody lead—
one for each shot
meant to leave you dead
in the shooting gallery of the heart.

## Sixty Years of Mondays

In the theater of happily ever after
the demolition crew ignites the charges.
Shards of shattered window glass
punctuate the back of every seat.
Cellists play a funeral dirge
as *What Is* delivers the eulogy
for everything you hoped life would be.

You have missed the program's start
due in part to the mismatched shoes
at the foot of your bed
and that sobering revelation
in the dressing mirror
of the threadbare tux
your body has become.

It is too late to exchange your ticket,
to rearrange your strange and scrambled thoughts,
and plot a life that makes more sense.
Instead, you end up here,
attempting to measure infinity
with a ragged piece of string:
sixty years of Mondays
spent on hands and knees
crawling up and down the empty aisles
in the abandoned factory of unattainable dreams
nudging the small red ball of the soul
past the luminous clock dial of night
toward some ill-defined vision of eternity
where the silent god who shaped you
and set you adrift
fingers the essential parts of you
he greedily keeps for himself
deep in the pockets of his overcoat.

Your intentions were once white museum walls,
but the graffitti of missed opportunity
now hangs in place of the art
you dreamed you would someday create.

And don't even pretend you believe in love,
that refuge of the fool,
that uncharted country of the always lost
where compass needles spin
in constant indecision.

Perhaps there could have been more than this,
perhaps you pursued the parts
at the expense of the sum.
No matter, you are playing to an empty house now.
The dirge you hear is clearly meant for you:
whatever it was you could have been or done
matters less now than what you have become.

## Greenhouse Battleground

*for Carol Clark-Williams*

Inside this miniature Eden of whitewashed glass
petaled cannons flash,
silent rockets explode
in bursts of searing color.
Raging conflagrations
of red and gold and green
lay swaths of ruthless splendor
where a lifeless landscape
once had been.

**Laundry as Life #2**

One day it might occur to you
that no one really cares
about that woe-filled laundry basket
you lug around life's laundromat.

Oh, some will say they do
in that distracted way an acquaintance does,
but in truth, he has merely grown weary
of listening to the annoying thud
of his own unbalanced laundry load
banging around the spin cycle
inside the washing machine of his head.

## Sedna*

What did I know?
The world you offered—
insubstantial as a promise—
had no foundation
to support the stuffed animals
of a young girl's dreams.

What defense did I have
against your desire?
Its raptors hunted down my innocence
and shredded every tender wish,
before transforming themselves into angry fists.

What did I learn?
I learned how not to flinch
at each stroke of knife on bone,
even at being thrown, joint by joint,
into the blood-mottled coffin of the sea.

I know how difficult it must be
for you to understand
the gratitude I feel for your gifts:
for this dark dream-world of fishes,
and most of all,
for having nothing—ever again—
to do with man.


*In Eskimo mythology, queen of the land of the dead under the sea.

**Unfinished**

> *for Gwyn McVay*

These poems, like birds,
clamor for nourishment.
Until they are fully fledged,
the spectre of natural selection looms.
No matter how many feathers
I rip from my breast
and offer up in sacrifice
so that each greedy creature might survive,
some will die.

And when one of them falters,
I spread its white winding sheet
across the emergency room
of the refrigerator door,
open my box of crayons,
and color in the dull gray
of its fading cheeks with Rose Madder
a touch of Peach,
and keep constant vigil until I am certain
there is no more breath left.

> *O Babushka, I still can hear you reciting*
> *the unfinished blue poem of each baby*
> *you laid to rest in a row*
> *along the weary backyard fence.*

Long ago I drove far away
from the weather-scoured prairies
toward this strange land of Pennsylvania,
where crosses for the dead bloom gratefully
like stark wildflowers
standing along the highways' dark and littered berms.

*O Babushka, please make me apples and tea
one more time
like I was a child.*

Now I am driving down this road,
with the ghost of a poem in my head,
to a place where one of those
lonely paint-chipped crosses grow,
and I will speak the poem's name like a prayer,
sadly whisper "unfinished,"
and dedicate these lines to the life
that was also left unfinished
here on this spot
not so very long ago.

**Parent Trap**

They are drinking beer and smoking cigarettes,
this parent circle, asses parked on logs,
their voices and laughter dimming
around the campfire's weary embers.

Their children are sleepy,
beginning to torment the younger ones
because it's what kids do when left too long
to their own devices.

I am hiding beneath my father's steamboat-size Pontiac,
somewhere between the parents' impotent threats
and the kids' incessant need to push.

At that moment I vow to avoid parenthood's trap
and swear an oath to the universe
where I am a rogue star
drifting now through life's already turbulent cosmology
inside my skin's awkward spacesuit
with no concept whatsoever
of what *future* means,
but I figure it has something to do
with beer and cigarettes and a bone-deep dissatisfaction
with us—the by-products of their desires
and the impediments to their dreams.

### *Kristallnacht*

The smell of burnt coffee
fills the cafe air,
cappuccino snakes hiss
rich clouds of steamed milk
behind a copper-covered counter.
The ceaseless sound of cellular voices
adds to the background noise,
and a liquid crystal Hi-Def drip
dulls the pain
flowing through the eyes and ears
slipping into the nodding brain,
while newspaper and magazine pages turn
and a burning world is explained away
in sound bytes
by blue suits with power ties.

Outside windows fogged by steam,
a car explodes,
a village dies.
Screaming mouths fill up with sand,
eyes relinquish dreams
and surrender one-by-one
all the things they once believed were true.

You hear the echo
of change as it passes through,
the martial cadence of hob-nailed soles
on black leather boots.
They are waving the flag at you again,
assaulting the air with their cheers,
their loud hallelujahs.

So you give them what they want:
your silence, your allegiance,
you let them read your mail
and listen when you are on the phone.

When they ask for more
you give your daughters and your sons—
no price is too high to feel secure.

And if you listen carefully
when you are bundled
in your safe and tranquil beds you might
make out the distant sound
of windows breaking in the night.

## Love and Music 1: Blue Notes

*for Le Hinton*

Blue notes
kinda blue
a solo saxophone
Coltrane all alone
white shirt drenched in sweat
inside the holy halo of the spot
all those soulful notes so hot
pouring like molten brass
into the instant air
there for a heartbeat then not.

Blue notes
our kind of blue
hazy melody
you and me in perfect time
the sweet music of our life
deep and slow
a kiss-soft moan
dark and light
the music and the flesh
blending fleetingly into one pure song
too delicate a piece, too spontaneous and brief
for our lips and ears and fingers
to catch its magic,
make it linger a few beats longer.

Blue notes
these intricate blue harmonies
of a love supreme
slowly unravel,
the spaces between grow dissonant
your voice fades into blue
it travels these empty rooms and sounds to me
like footsteps walking away.

My fingers can't play the melody
in quiet smoke-filled darkness
they fumble desperately to find the key
and give voice
to this silent scream working its way
around midnight,
around the wreckage,
out through the blue labyrinth
of my soul.

**Part II
The Boilermaker's Daughter**

"You must always be wary
of what you pray and wish,
for neither god nor fate
seems to hold very dear
the fragile cargo of our dreams."

## The Boilermaker's Daughter

I was nineteen, a lifetime ago,
half mad from crickets
and the haunting fear
of a future without exit doors.
During those long years of war,
I danced alone in the attic
above the clatter of mealtime dishes
and the endless chatter of younger sisters
who broke or stole the few fine things
I once had called my own.

Like Rapunzel
I waited with my face against the glass
peering past that unpaved lane
to the moonlit highway that promised escape.
I strained to read
the endless motion of grass and air and trees,
strained to decipher the features
of the man
I prayed fate would send to rescue me.

And this is what happens
when you finally catch
the capricious eye of fate:
you get a roll of wooden nickels
and a roller coaster ride through life
with a carefree handsome soldier
who has your longing in his sights.

How could I have foreseen,
on my lonely vigil,
the reckless path his love would take,
or the whispered litany of promises
he never failed to break—
or the lifetime of empty nights?

And how could I have calculated the countless blows
a hungry heart might have to take
before it chose to turn to stone
to inure itself to pain?

## The Boilermaker's Daughter Speaks of Madness

During the inquisition of the day
my heart kept time with the clock,
the bottomless cup filling up with hours
while I watched the slow curl of paper
lose its grip
on the sanity of walls.

It drove me mad
to sit inside the velvet pocket of night,
to listen to the hungry teeth of mice
tunneling through the house.

When all of you were at peace
in sleep's reassuring arms
I would sneak out back
with a box of blue-tipped kitchen matches,
and soak a rag in gasoline.

I could clearly see
the unfolding silent movie of my crime
projected in black and white
on the star-pinned sky:
shadows moving in a dream,
full moon eyes in the chill damp air,
my open mouth,
its soundless scream,
the nightgowned goblin
dancing wildly on bare feet
pouring gasoline on the wooden treads
of the back porch stairs.
And me,
lighting the rag like a fuse.

## Valediction of the Boilermaker's Daughter

Still gazing out windows after all these years,
that ghost of a road
flowing dimly into moonlight...

What happened to time?—
First, its tedious pace when I was young,
rolling up behind me now like a wave.
I am running in sand...

What brutal miracles
I have worked with these hands—
created desperate children living desperate lives:
a daughter who no longer speaks to me,
a son I never see—
O, I have given back doubly
all that was given me.

That night before my wedding,
instead of outlining the role
of a dutiful wife,
I wish Mother had simply said
this life is the alternative
to happily-ever-after.

Ah!—goddamn them all...

## The Boilermaker's Daughter Speaks to Her Son from the Other Side

What could I tell you
of the heart's stark exile?
Where would I begin
to teach you how its desperate fingers reach,
how its solitude lingers like a scar
upon the soul's tender plain?
O, my curious creation,
who else but a mother could demonstrate
the damnation of a life best unlived?

I taught you the catechism of shame,
the frightful grammar of despair
and the endless poetry of pain—
far better to be crippled
by those you love
than to be maimed
by the considerable power of surprise.

I tried to show you where danger hides,
my little fool, and
like a mother cat
bringing back wounded creatures
to teach her offspring how to kill,
I showed you where
the vulnerable parts of the heart reside.

But you persist
in believing that love can override
your nature's dark engine.
And *this* will be the punishment
for your crime:
a life of hard labor spent
doing time on the chain gang of regret.

You have always been clay
in my lovely fists,
even though you continue to insist
that long ago you left me far behind.

You were my first and finest creation.
There is no escape.
And I weep with pride each time
I gaze upon the beautiful gargoyle
these angry hands have shaped.

## The Boilermaker's Daughter Speaks to Her Daughter on the Other Side

Through all those wasted years we battled,
I knew how hard you struggled
to be free of me.
And the day I died,
I won't deny it pained me to hear
that sigh
issue from your unburdened soul.

But things are very different here.
It is important for you to know
that there is no salvation,
no eternity of tormenting flame.
Only guilt and regret remain
like a never-ending movie that reminds us
we should have been better people
when we were both alive.

In this place there are no lies:
all the secret rooms of your life
are now unlocked
and I can clearly see
the devious furniture of all your schemes.

Of course, I am also aware
that the closely-guarded vault of my designs
has revealed its twisted treasure.
But there is no profit in this prize,
no measure of advantage
for either of us to claim.
Instead, we are required
to set aside the myths and lies
we have created and cultivated
to hide our own imperfections,
to blame each other
for the failure of our lives.

It seems somehow fitting punishment
that we should stand here, together again,
where we will be equally judged
before the impartial eye.

And what is most important
is not that I was a mother
and you were my daughter,
but that each of us has been found guilty
for all that we have squandered.

**Epilog: In the Wake**

I had wished her here
a thousand times
in my darkest thoughts
when I was a child
reeling under her angry fists.
But now the moment had no fuel
to ignite the cold gray ash
of our abused and turbulent past.

All I wanted before that frigid day
was the cleansing gift of my outrage:
to hear the eruption of my voice
echoing off that mountain range
of granite stones.
I wanted all those other resting souls
to know who was moving into
their neighborhood.

Oh, here was a lifetime
of humiliation and dread
wanting to be tapped like a keg,
to be purged and spilled
across this snow-covered
landscape of the dead.

But none of those emotions
of place and time
could claim dominance
and so were cancelled out—
gone, like she was.

I found myself stunned instead,
wondering how a force her size,
with all her anger and violence,
could be reduced

to a pile of ashes
and crammed inside such a small container,
and how it all could sit there
so quietly upon the ground.

And we—the ones she could not kill,
staring at the ragged circle
that was to be her grave—
stood silently
in awe of the power her presence—
even in this altered form—
still could generate.

**Part III:**

**Ghost in the Hallway**

"But there are fault lines in the heart
beyond love's great power to repair..."

## At 3 O'Clock in the Morning

The kitchen clock ticks toward dawn,
thunder and lightning bluster,
hustling wind and rain along the streets.
All of time and space
gather with us here
on these wobbly chairs,
on countertops and windowsills
as we speak of art and poetry we have made—
both of us wondering
just how much luck it might take
for any of it
to live longer than we will.

## Lorca's Daughter

It is there in your voice,
your choice of words:
the exotic cadence
of that sacred heart-music,
those Andalusian melodies
on which the legacy of Flamenco
has been nursed.

In the sanctuary of your verse
your words are guitars and castanets
that reach beyond the poems of others
and sow passionate seeds
across the flat white plains of my ears
so that even I can hear
the desperate muse
as she prays to *you*
for inspiration.

**Sleeping with the Muse**

Light is leaking through
a broken slat in the window blind.
Venus fades in the winter morning sky.
Sleep's gentle mask rests upon your face
as I lie here bathed in the grace of your gifts.

Seeing you like this,
it is difficult to imagine
the tangled skeins of past violation and pain
knitting themselves into inspiration
beneath your gently-sloping breast.

There are prayers to be whispered
at moments such as this,
but the amens and hallelujahs
that stumble against my stuttering tongue
fail to measure their significance.

Even though no poems
were written last night upon this bed,
I am most grateful to you
for providing my tortured head
a tranquil place to rest.

**Duet for Cello and Piano**

*for Barbara DeCesare*

Rain-drenched sonatas
spill from piano keys.
Untamed melodies explode from your fingertips
bursting into flame
lingering no longer
than those first tentative sips of love ever did.

It is for love's intimate music that we kiss
that we kill
that we are willing to become
desperados of the heart.

This is the part we live for:
skating the thin forbidding ice
tracing lavish figure-eights
around the hungry mouth of death,
and the awful leaning in
toward that ultimate kiss—
the mutual blood-letting
the exquisite pain—
because nothing else comes this close to love.

I will be your cello.
I will sing for you,
you will burn for me.

**Land and Sea**


I am drowning here on dry land,
and though you are not required to rescue me,
your waters claw at the sand
piling up shells and jewels of polished glass
because it is in your nature
to give everything you have.

It was an old man's folly brought me here
to be made a fool by time's swift undertow,
to think that one so old and bound to the land
still might swim
in your warm and seductive tides.

It is not your fault.
I understand that your heart is large,
but you cannot be expected
to carry the cargo
of every drowning man who, one day, finds himself
falling in love with the sea.

**Ghost in the Hallway**

If this were a movie
you would be cast as the ghost in the hallway,
the hazy image on the still life of the mirror glass.
I would be only half
the half-a-man I appear to be,
made less substantial by passing time—
an almost ghost—
yet still too solidly of this world
to cross the frontier into yours.

And though we appear together on screen,
there is no dialog,
only Nadja's solo violin
embroidering the background of each scene.
The audience might believe
there was some way
for one of us to part the membrane,
because they have always been led
to expect such from this art.
But there are fault lines in the heart
beyond love's great power to repair,
and real barriers of time and circumstance
where there is the chance that two spirits
will forever remain apart.

> *There is a space inside my arms*
> *that is shaped like you,*
> *and when I hold my hands like a nest,*
> *your face could rest like a bird*
> *in my palms.*
> *At night I am transformed into the shoreline*
> *defined by the invisible harbor of your body,*
> *and before I drift to sleep*
> *my open hand cups the talisman*
> *of your breast.*

It is true, I want too much.
I always have.
Eventually, you will glide past me
like the wind as morning comes,
and disappear down a path among the trees.

And here the movie ends, as it must,
perhaps in a wide shot:
an empty, dusty country road,
the sun rising from behind a hill,
the ghost of the moon hovering
above the fog-draped trees.

## Love and Music 2: Duet

*for Rebecca Gonzalez*

In the aftermath of love's last hurricane
I am mending the heart's broken furniture.
I am cleaning up the debris,
learning to be enough
in night's celibate exile.

Sirens scream
beneath my open windows
making these dark unhappy streets
unfit places for love and commitment to meet.

But up here
above all that three-alarm calamity
a saxophone plays quietly for me,
its holy tune a different shade of blue
spanning time and place:
me here, someone out there
both still out of synch
yet inching closer
across the karmic concert all of space
until our solos at last become duet.

# Part IV
# Dismantling a Life

"…notice how it seems
you were never really there at all"

## Artist's Statement

*for Adam Cowan*

In this still life
I arrange precious objects
and paint them as I see them.
Though blemished in time's unforgiving glow
I hope they will also have significance
for someone pausing to examine
what another's life has meant.

But how does one place value
on what has accumulated:
these jars and candlesticks,
the half-full carafe of wine,
the bruises mottling the banana's yellow skin?

What table covering spread beneath
will unite the themes
of joy and dreams and unhappiness?
And what light is best?
That from a south-facing window
or the hard, uncompromising glare
of an unshaded overhead?

What is it I hope to lay out
on clean white canvas fields
that might resemble a map,
or the history of some ordinary fellow's
struggle to avoid anonymity?

Whatever it is remains elusive,
or perhaps lays quite still and clear,
a testament to one man's attempt
at living the art of his life.

Whatever resonates, whatever suffers
from poor placement or over-painting
will have to withstand scrutiny.
Whatever it is, I have come to realize
that it is a poor painter
who blames his brushes.

## Wedding Portrait--1971

She wanted "Bridge Over Troubled Waters"
sung at our wedding
but I said no,
conscious of how even something like a song could jinx.
And while reciting vows I had written
I struggled to connect those words
to what I was feeling,
except that what I was feeling
had nothing to do with two people
who had recognized the drowning in each other
and against all advice
had booked passage on a ship
destined to be torpedoed.

There were friends and family
a cake in a college town
and a ceremony that defied convention—
not much else planned
beyond that Sunday afternoon between semesters.

After one last toast to our happiness
everyone left a little drunk,
some were envious that only I
would get to test drive those killer curves—
curves I already knew by heart—
beneath that velvet midnight blue wedding dress.

There was the trip to Paris we never took,
the young ex-patriates
we were never destined to become—
she improving her French among the natives,
me writing stories and poems
at outdoor cafes, my pages held in place
beneath a stack of chipped china saucers.

But this is not what made our unhappiness.
I think it was the going back.
Once we understood that marriage
had so many more ways to divide than to unite
we retreated to that small town and the families
we had wished to leave behind
because neither of us had a better plan,
and the romance of romance
had no buoyancy.

It all came down stick by stick,
and we helped it some:
she in the heat of other men,
me standing still occupying indecision's
well-furnished living room
staring out its windows late at night watching,
waiting for that one night
when she didn't return home
to signal the end.

**Cat's Cradle**

The air conditioner is emphysemic
from the scourge of second-hand smoke,
and you are convinced the juke box
is broken when "Proud Mary"
plays for the eighth consecutive time.

The woman sitting beside you
has too much make-up around her eyes.
The desperate butterfly of her fingers flutters
from her hair to her drink
to her cigarette lighter and back again.
She has coke dust on her nose
and tattoos on her thighs:
one of which reads "Heaven"
with an arrow pointing up
toward some dark promise of paradise
beyond the hem of her black leather mini-skirt.

You forget whose idea it was
to meet here in this torture chamber,
to sit among giant video screens
and attempt to talk
over the amplified enthusiasm of stadium screams
and the testosterone-driven voices
of drunken young men in three-piece suits
looking to provoke a fight
or hoping to get lucky—or both.

You left your youth—like extravagant tips—
in similar places
one double bourbon and cigarette at a time.
And now you wonder if
the Holy Grail you were pursuing then
is the same as that which eludes
these present-day crusaders
chasing after *La Dolce Vita*.

The facile fingers of experience
have only just begun
to weave the intricate cat's cradle
of these frenetic lives.
One day some will realize,
despite the pressures that drove them here,
it would be better to have back these hours
or just half the money spent.
But today will not be the day
they are obliged to learn
the weight of every stone,
the price in relation to the cost,
or the proportion of profit
compared to what was lost.

**Title Search**


The Iroquois once used this land
as a path between the river
and the cathedral of coniferous trees.
When the settlers came—
scattering like glowing embers from the hand of god—
ablaze with a mission to prosper and dominate,
the Indians were driven off—or killed—
and their great gods were chopped down
and burned out along with the trees—
every trace of them devoured
by generations of cattle,
replacing ritual and mystery
with the mundane commerce of milk
and animal husbandry.

Not long after the last bachelor farmer's passing
the old dairy farm
became a munitions dump
for the excess ordinance of a war
that had run out of enemies.
When the government was through with it
the creaking vehicles retreated,
leaving behind hastily-erected barbed wire fences
and "No Trespassing" signs.

Eventually the patient land healed itself—
leveled the buildings,
settled over the bullets and the bombs
as it had the granite genealogy
of that original farming family—
closing over those old infected wounds
with the gently-rolling scar tissue of soil
stitched together with chaotic sutures
of milk weed, ivy and Queen Anne's Lace.

Now Monarch butterflies silently explode
from the silk-lined rockets of milk weed pods
scattering across the landscape
like fire-glazed stones
dropped from the burning palms of god.

## In the Grotto of the Saint

A child weeps at the wailing wall,
his fingers and feet
missed the bus that brought him here
along with all those nuns in civilian clothes.

There is a wicker basket
in the arthritic hands of a half-blind acolyte
who started out a pederast
but found god hiding amid the chewing gum
beneath his seat
on a midnight bus bound for Akron,
that holy city of tires.

Onlookers explore the mine shafts of their pockets
for guilty coins to feed the basket's greedy maw
to buy indulgence for their mortal sin
of perfect health in this garden
where cripples sprout and grow
into the grotesque flowers of god's untidy will.

The saint who found this place
instead of those wayward sheep she was seeking,
she who hallucinated the mother of god,
the archangel of god,
or some other sacred emissary,
she is gone
dead so long ago
that no one who knew her only as a child—
without her purple mantle of miracle—
no one is alive to say out loud
or even to whisper contemptuously,
*"she was such a strange kid,*
*none of us ever put much stock*
*in what she said."*

## The Dealer

But right now
the doctor fusses with his tie
as he studies a sheet
of neatly-typed single-spaced
words and numbers.

He is dealing with diagnosis now,
and what he really wants
is to be the dealer
at a Vegas Black Jack table
who plays for "The House,"
but really wants to slide you
the ace of hearts
off the bottom of the deck
to go with that lonely face card
buried in front of you.

He wants this to be your lucky day,
perhaps the luckiest day of your life
because so much depends on chance.
But for now he scans the numbers,
calculates the odds
like an actuary.
He is puzzled that he did not see this coming.

So instead of that bold red ace,
he watches your face as you fold
when he tells you that
not only have you run out of money,
but it appears that soon
you will run out of time.

It is the one part of his job he hates:
watching people go for broke
wagering everything on hope—
the weakest hand of all.

## No Such Place as Here

*for Rich Hemmings*

I want to be a river,
giving birth to myself on a glacial shelf
high on the granite spine
of some western mountain range,
gathering my strength from tributaries
swollen by seasonal rains.

I want to be a river
carving canyons and gorges
as I forge my way toward my destination.
I want to carry boulders in my belly
and grind them to pebbles and sand.
I want to fashion islands
and riverbanks with my rage.
My voice will mock the thunder,
I will steal my color from the sky,
and shatter the pretentious sun
and the modest moon
into a thousand scattered pieces
upon the mirror of my back.

I want to be a river,
to feed a nation,
to ferry its commerce across my shoulders.
I want to press like a threat
against the concrete breasts of dams
and drive massive iron turbines
powering cities and farms and industries.
I want to form boundaries
between states and nations,
be called by different names on opposite shores
and hold opposing dreams and aspirations.

I want to be a river
instead of being stranded here
out of gas in the breakdown lane
alongside life's interstate.
I want to be driven
by the river's single-minded resolve:
to go,
to be delivered by the act of moving—
become an angel of motion—
never remaining in one place
frozen in the face of one's own fear,
wrapped in the straightjacket of loss and despair.

I want to be a river because,
to a river, there is no such place as *here*.

**Expedition**

The woman at the next table
stares at a map
in a battered Atlas.
She bites into a bran muffin
and chews slowly to hide the fact
her lips move
when she reads the names
of towns and cities.

She is unaware
I know her
and can plainly see
the missing pieces
in the ragged fortress around her heart.
It appears,
the way her eyes dart from the page
past the still life framed by the café's glass
and back again,
that she has lost her way
and might think, perhaps, this book of maps
could lead her back
to before the hiss of hospital doors,
before the mind numbing trance
induced by endless fluid-drips,
before the slow-motion dissolve
of her lover's spirit and body
into memory's poorly-lit morgue.

I see her nod,
and she begins to turn each page with resolve,
as if the route were now abundantly clear,
that one of these blue-shaded regions—
bordered by those in pink and green—
contains the magic topography of change.
And leaving behind the Atlas,
the half-eaten muffin
and cold cup of tea,

she is gone like a moment,
gone, perhaps, off to explore
the *terra incognita*
beyond the frightful shore line
of all that must be left behind.

**Monument**

On winter nights
colder now beneath the weight
of accumulated years stacked like cans
on a grocery shelf,
the dull linoleum aisle of days
slips away in the feeble half-light
filtering through
the past's smeared plate glass windows.

She is always there
at the end of the aisle
at the end of each day:
that curly explosion of red hair
her smile a constant bubble—
a miniature sun—
the twin full moons of her breast
floating on the horizon
of this fading blue planet
I have created
from the rubble of wrong choices,
from the bone yard of indecision—
a monument to missed opportunity.

**Laundry Service**

There are teeth and vomit
on the parking lot
outside the laundromat door.

In the lint trap of a dryer
I find a condom,
a wadded-up kleenex,
and a plea for help
crudely printed in chocolate-sparkle lipstick
on a fabric softener sheet.

It is Sunday morning,
we are attending the sacred mass
of sheets and socks and underwear—
*Holy Father, hear our prayers:*
*cleanse our souls and these soiled clothes,*
*pray for us sinners toiling here.*

Surrounded by washing machines,
assailed by the muted tones
of iPod tunes
leaking from the amphitheater of troubled skulls,
I am growing restless here
among all these dirty clothes.

We stand, faces pressed against the dryers' glass,
beseeching heaven.
We are agitated souls,
we are already dead,
our sins spin before our eyes
and we are mesmerized
by the pointless folly
of all we've done to change our fate.

It is too late, we fear.

We are not evil people here,
condemned to an eternity
of suds and solitude,
but, nonetheless, here we are—
Sunday after Sunday—
lugging our sins in laundry baskets
down to this river
to beat them against repentance's stone.

And when we leave,
each of us leaves alone,
washed in the new light,
each sin atoned.

# Reckoning

*for Dustin Nispel*

My hapless path is strewn with poems
and too-few acts of kindness.
Perhaps the Hansel part of me
truly believed these impermanent landmarks
could one day guide me back,
back to all that had been
too eagerly bartered away
in order to feel secure.

This notebook I carry
grows light as a wish.
After all these years
pages flutter and fly away
at an alarming pace
and disappear
like the crisply-defined ideals of youth.
And my pen is nearly empty,
poems slowly bleed
from the artery of its disillusioned heart—
wounded long ago by compromise.

In this realm of harsh surprise
beneath an unresolved sky
regret's imposing clouds gather,
attempting to obscure
what must now be clearly seen.

Who was I then I am not now?

It is nearly the hour of reckoning:
the final accountant awaits
with his black debit book
somewhere down time's darkening corridor
where, one day,
light will lose the power to find me.

One final task remains:
the summing up,
the calculation of gain and loss,
the value of choice
weighed against its cost.

What was it I held then
that I have lost?

## Blue Trucks

*"She is gone in blue trucks painted with secrets"—*
*Bob Kaufman*

At night, blue with the sound
of laboring trucks,
you watch the street light transform itself
into the spaces between venetian blinds
and crash silently
against the peeling paper
of your bedroom walls.

As you stare at the ceiling—
that Milky Way of abandoned dreams
scrambling like confused comets
with no way home—
you realize everything you ever wanted sounds like rain,
resembles bad paintings
jammed into the back corner of a cluttered garage.

No wine, no cigarettes,
a crotchload of useless love
suspended between what you remember
and what you will never learn.

There's a reason they paint "good-byes" blue.
They drive them around in blue trucks
with noisy brakes and loud mufflers
so you will never forget
the sound of those words,
never grow complacent in their absence,
so you will always recognize their approach
when you hear the backfire,
the grind of downshifting gears
just before they turn the corner
onto the street where you live.

## The Stone Witch

To the neighborhood kids
she was the old stone witch
whose gaze was known to turn
wayward boys and stray dogs
into solid stone.

Nevertheless we would venture out,
like a miniature army,
and crawl across the night-damp grass
to spy on that frozen figure dressed in black—
framed in the living room window glass
like a specimen—
sitting severely there
in her caned-back wheelchair.

It was those immobile eyes,
their hawk-like glare
and that untamed nest of white hair
that brought us out night after night—
like a triple-dare—
to explore the uncertain coastline
of our own individual fear.

One night her husband caught us,
and we were far too surprised to run,
as if our feet had already begun
their fearful transformation to stone.
He spoke kindly—
called by name the two of us he knew—
and one-by-one we stood, quietly shamed,
vaguely aware that our behavior
had crossed some accepted line.

Sensing this he invited us in
and offered each
the golden gift of an apple

to assuage our sin,
then led us into the living room
to formally meet his wife.

We presented ourselves,
mumbling our names
in that awkward manner of guilty boys.
But she did not acknowledge or move,
neither did her gaze change any of us to stone.

I was the last in line to leave,
and at the door
the old man touched my shoulder.
"I believe she was glad," he said,
to have boys in the house again."
Something in his voice
conveyed to me a sadness
it would take me years to comprehend:
that of children sentenced to early graves,
and of parents who have been condemned
to remain and endure.

**Prelude**

Insubstantial as smoke
climbing autumn air,
softer than bird song,
light as night's patient hands
tucking in the weary day,
I am hovering above your body's abundant plane
neither of the air
nor of the ground—
suspended
like a dream—
waiting like a prayer
for the invocation of your lips.

## The Star of Film Noir


This is where you long to be—
dressed in a rumpled trench coat,
sporting a crumpled felt fedora,
a Lucky Strike jutting aggressively
from the corner of your George Raft mouth—
projected at 24 frames per second
in black and white
on every tiny neighborhood theater screen
where you ever watched a movie.

You are living someone else's life now:
resourceful in dark alleys littered with danger,
quick to anger, with a noir-style quip
for either the villain or the crooked cop
when he cocks the hammer of his deadly repartée.
You savor fear's acid flavor,
the way it lingers in the back of your throat
like a neat cheap whiskey
with three X's on the label.

And because there is always a dame
with a gimmick for turning the tables,
you want her to have legs to die for,
since the odds are you probably will.
But if you don't,
the odds are better that near the end of the picture
you'll wind up face down
between those lovely legs
wrapped ecstatically
around your head.

It doesn't matter that you lack creativity,
that you never conceived of—or carried out—
a bank heist or a double-cross.

In spite of triumph or loss

there are no real surprises
because it is all laid out for you:
everything you need to say and do
is neatly typed on flimsy blue pages—
changes in action and dialog
delivered fresh to you on the set each day
by the nicotine-stained fingers
of the faithful script girl's hand.

So your honor may be lost or saved,
and the heroine may not love you in the end,
but at the very least,
when you walk away—wounded and alone—
something will be resolved,
someone will be transformed.

**Pirate**

I suppose I should be grateful to you
for hastening the inevitable.
We all know these shipwrecks of the heart
are better borne by younger men
who are strong enough
to swim away from the undertow.

I have no sympathy, though,
for the pirate who does not comprehend
the basic laws of his trade:
that she who has been taken
can also be taken away.

I have seen you drowning
in land-locked taverns and bars,
and I have watched you stagger
toward the comforting arms of the sea,
and sink to your knees upon the sand
at the very same spot
where she marooned my heart
on the island of her infidelity.

I hear the empty bottles
of your prayers
clinking out to sea at night,
but neither water nor sand
can save you now.

And as for me?
I will not save you either
by saying it's all right.

## Pictures

*for Barbara Rath*

What do I do with these pictures,
the ones inside my head:
my sister sprawled upon a hospital bed
tethered by plastic tubes and wires
to bottles
and bleating machines that keep her breathing
because the severed circuitry
between her brain and spine no longer can?

How does all this fit?
Into whose grand design?
And who would risk rolling those dice?
Against what odds?
You can't have anything you desire,
not love or happiness,
but you can end up a stalk of celery
after being T-boned into limbo
by an SUV on an icy highway
five miles from the safety of your home.

Our father huddles there,
looking all of his eighty years,
slumped in a hospital wheelchair
signing papers
absolving responsibility,
speaking all the while,
believing she can hear his voice
above the gasps of that laboring machine
forcing air deep into her lungs.

And I want to say
we'd like her to stay if she can
and it's okay to go of she must.
But I am inert, face to face

with everything I fear,
wanting to run because I always have,
my brain like a crime scene photographer,
images multiplying like a disease:
*the blue and yellow pattern on her gown*
*the clock-like clear fluid drip*
*the tube in her throat*
*our father keeps on speaking*
*doctors and nurses huddle in a corner*
*as if hatching a conspiracy*
*I can't speak*
*I want to run*
*but my feet are stuck*
*to the black and white checkerboard*
*of the hospital tile*
*the clear fluid drips*
*my father scratches his name on forms*
*snow eddies outside the window*
*doctors and nurses glance over their shoulders*
*whispering, gesturing, their vague incantations*
*keeping time with the respiration machine*
*a snowplow rattles outside on the street…*
Christ! It's so cold in here.

# Yeti

*(After reading Szymborska's "Notes from a Nonexistent Himalayan Expedition")*

Yes, these are the Himalayas,
kingdom of rock and clouds and snow
where eons ago the moon
relaxed her tentative grip
and gently drifted into space.

Down there, you tell me,
you have poetry and music and art,
that you have devised a way
to cut time's continuous thread
into individual days.
Up here I listen to the wind's symphony.
I have memorized the endless saga of ice,
and wandered half-blind
across snow's ruthless canvas.

You ask me to reconsider,
as if I would go back
to that moment when our paths diverged
in order to merge again
with the family of man.
But sometimes
I watch your needlepoints of light
tattoo night's tender flesh,
and am grateful never to have known fear.

Perhaps it is a life of utter despair,
unadorned by illusions of culture and civility.
There is no reason for hope up here,
the fundamental struggle
is so clearly drawn, so crisply defined,
like the stiletto-sharp edge
of each punishing breath of air.

There is no relief anywhere,
and my isolation
rages down these mountains
like an avalanche.

## Weather Report

That Sunday everything broke:
the uncluttered table of our lives
divided in one casual stroke.

We were sharing coffee at the outdoor café,
muffins and butter—
neither of us uttering a word
through the long minutes of our usual
Sunday matinee—
when rust-tinged petals
began dropping from the bloom.

I suppose I should have noticed this,
considering how late it was
in the afternoon of our relationship.

But I was thinking of that morning,
how without warning, you let slip
I needed to lose some weight—
that walking was great exercise.
And it was no surprise when you said
you would be working late with Tom
at the office again next week.

It was then
you closed the cover on that novel
you had long-since lost interest in,
and flicked the remnant
of your half-smoked cigarette
onto the freshly-mulched flower bed.

Gazing absently at the cloudless sky
you sighed and shook your head:
"Looks like rain."

**Stopped Clocks**


The tenements suck light from streetlamps
filtering it back
through broken windows
like bullet holes
in their gritty brick torsos.

Everything is victim here,
wounded
in the drive-by shooting of futility.

Hope lies buried somewhere over there
where trees once grew
and pigeons marched and flew
in cluttered circles.

These summer nights
hold the heat like a blanket,
tucking its woolen hem
tightly in around the mattress
of our despair.
Our open mouths gasp like fish
sucking at the hot dry air
struggling to keep the stone of life
secure in our throats
lodged in our hearts
because it is all we have for now.

Gunshots in the distance
a siren sounds
disoriented feet trying to outrace the verdict
of that tiny lead mushroom
he carries like a deadly telegram.

Staggering from shadows
struggling for breath
his knees unlock
spilling him like garbage
at the alley's dark mouth.

We have witnessed it all before.
There is no sense of urgency,
no outrage, no shock:
he is death's taxi now,
his eyes already filling up
with stopped clocks.

## Home

*for R.M. Rath*

"There's no place like home," the samplers quote.
But I have moved so often in my life
there is nowhere I've been
that ever seemed like home.

Each settling had a feel of its own,
came with an assortment
of memories I unwrapped, one-by-one,
like gifts.
Yet no one spot ever quite fit
like the comfortable slippers
I imagined home to be.

Rented houses in new cities
echoed the sound of my voice
from the empty box canyons of their rooms,
but had no answers
when I asked: "Am I home?"

At night my dreams inhabit
other structures, other towns I have known,
but can neither settle down
nor draw the sheets of comfort tightly enough
around them to say they're home.

There is no Atlas I can find
with maps and grids
to guide my heart and thoughts
across the rivers, over the mountains
and boundaries
to that one place
where everything remains
exactly as I remember
no matter how long it's been
since last I was there.

**Inside the Mirror**


There are reasons you prefer not to look into mirrors:
there is more to it
than you simply looking back
appraising a fresh haircut,
calculating the inherent power
in the color and stripe of a new necktie.
There are sins in there, too,
hiding behind your eyes,
trapped on that ice sheet of a space
with no sense of dimension.

That vampire inside you
has no wish to know
that his soul is condemned to float
above the ground, below the clouds,
wandering forever in that insubstantial land
where prayers and helpful hands
can never quite reach him.
And it is better not to be mesmerized
by the killer's guilty blue eyes
gazing back with murderous intent—
they do not buy your self-serving lies and equivocations.

You are defenseless inside
the mirror's simple dyslexia:
it is you in reverse—
you receding from everything
you ever thought you were,
from everything you ever hoped to be—
it is the overwhelming truth of ageing,
a snapshot of each dreadful stage of decomposition
reminding you that memory and self-deception
cannot survive on the translucent tundra
of its unforgiving stare.

The mirror is not swayed
by conventional notions of beauty.
It does not care to be kind.

## Love and Music 3: Casualties

Love and music
intimate as a solo saxophone
lovers alone
important as breath
in this whiskey-and-sweat
cigarette-smoke air.

Let each blue note
kiss your lips
as it lifts itself like a prayer
up from the incubator of your soul.

Let it be that first kiss,
the last kiss,
any one of a thousand kisses
you can't forget.

Let music be your lover,
your lover the music.
Listen when she whispers
in your ear.
Hear those fleeting words
form like a poem in your soul—
not in your head—
remember:
in love and music
the first casualty is always the heart.

**Risks**

*for Jeannie S.*

This December morning promises snow,
and though I despise this season's desolation
I am willing to risk its brittle power
to break living things
because I am breaking now
in jointed places
where action and reaction
rub against one another—
their dull friction a painful reminder
of how moving parts soon enough lose their power.

Whatever preceded is history,
is inaccessible and changeless now:
kisses never stolen,
my too-cautious hand on the waistband
of infidelity's risky underwear.

If she were here now
how much gray would infiltrate
her hair's once-abundant red meadow?
Would her face be all hard edges like mine,
a battlefield strewn with the corpses
of risks she was unwilling to chance?

Would she still find me dangerous
in that delicious way she once did
when I was married
and what we craved
scraped like agitated stone plates
across desire's unresolved landscape?
I can't even imagine a life with her now
just as I couldn't conceive of one without her then.

If kingdoms are lost
for the want of a nail,
I am uncertain as to how a risk accepted
affects the cosmic outcome of events,
but I do have some idea now
about the effects of a risk not taken.

**Son**

Something was always there between us:
at first the fruitbowl of your mother's belly,
then the automatic swish
of the Emergency Room door
and that score of doctors and nurses it took
to deny me the last decent chance
I had of seeing you
before the sterile green hush
of the undertaker's office where
he informed us that your remains
had already been "laid to rest"
in a shady corner of the family plot.

Today you would be older than I was
on the day you died,
and when you come to me in dreams
the city's streets are always too filled with people.
I hear what must be your voice,
but I cannot find your face in the crowd,
and no one responds when I call your name,
or else a loud voice replies: "Over here, Dad!
I'm over here, behind you!"
And when I turn around
the streets have emptied
and shop windows darken one-by-one
with a clicking sound that wakes me up,
and the moon-faced clock's steady ticking
admonishes me for straying once again
into that place
where all our disappointments reside.

The shadow pantomime of frenzied branches
reaches across the ceiling,
brushes against the moonlit walls
in this ghost theater of the night,
reminding me that once

I gathered together childhood photographs
of your mother and me.

Carefully I cut out the hair,
the ears, the lips and noses,
the mouths and the eyes
and tried to assemble a face
I could accept as yours
so that I might say hello
before I had to whisper good-bye.

## Dismantling a Life

It will be easier
if first you put the happiness inside a shoe box
and tightly tape on the lid and set it aside.
That way you will avoid any conflict
inherent in assessing the value
of the furniture
inside your life's cluttered rooms.

Don't stop to view any photographs,
this will only delay what must be done.
Just pack them away in the bottom of a box,
cover them with dish towels
or pillow cases—
accept that what you see in them
might cause regret
and only confuse the issue.

Place your few successes in a manilla envelope.
Write "Never To Be Opened" across the flap,
or perhaps just take it out to the backyard
and set it aflame
if you have the courage.
This will aid you in making
the tougher decisions that lie ahead.

Deal with the women next:
unwrap each carefully-packaged memory
and place it on the sill of an open window,
trust that sunlight and air
will complete what time could not.

Accept that the burden of your failures, your character flaws,
is too heavy for you to carry,
but nevertheless you will still be expected to drag it with you
wherever you go.

What remains can be swept into a pile
and left in the center of a room:
anonymous, ambiguous moments
that can't be traced back to you.

When you have finished,
walk through each room one last time,
listen to the hollow echo of your footsteps,
notice how it seems
you were never really there at all.

# Acknowledgments

Thanks are extended to the following publications in which the following poems appeared:

*Fledgling Rag:*
    "The Boilermaker's Daughter"
    "The Boilermaker's Daughter Speaks of Madness"
    "Valediction of the Boilermaker's Daughter"
    "The Boilermaker's Daughter Speaks to Her Son from the Other Side"
    "The Boilermaker's Daughter Speaks to Her Daughter on the Other Side"

*The Somerset Daily American—Poetry Corner:*
    "Home"

---

I wish to thank Carol Clark Williams and Barb DeCesare for their suggestions and assistance in preparing this manuscript for publication. Any shortcomings are due solely to my own bull-headedness and lack of technical proficiency.

Thanks are extended to Joanne Servansky for her keen proofreading eye.

Thanks to the R. E. Foundation and its efforts to spread the vision and power of poetry.

Thanks to Adam Cowan for the cover photograph, for his assistance in creating the collage that appears on the cover, and for his support and encouragement in all my artistic endeavors.

My heartfelt gratitude to Rebecca Gonzalez, V. Pres. of the MAS, who constantly inspires, for her efforts with the grunt work necessary to convert the Luddite miasma this manuscript was into its 21st Century counterpart.

Jeff Rath is the 2007 R.E. Foundation award winner for Outstanding Poetry and a Pushcart Prize nominee. His first collection of poetry was *The Waiting Room at the End of the World* (Iris G. Press, 2007).